MATHEMATICS DAY

T0080578

Shapes Around Us

Daniel Nunn

Raintree
Chicago, Illinois

www.capstonepub.com
Visit our website to find out more information about Heinemann-Raintree books.

To order:
Phone 800-747-4992
Visit www.capstonepub.com to browse our catalog and order online.

© 2012 Raintree
an imprint of Capstone Global Library, LLC
Chicago, Illinois

All rights reserved. No part of this publication may be reproduced or transmitted in any form or by any means, electronic or mechanical, including photocopying, recording, taping, or any information storage and retrieval system, without permission in writing from the publisher.

Edited by Daniel Nunn, Rebecca Rissman, and Sian Smith
Designed by Joanna Hinton-Malivoire
Picture research by Elizabeth Alexander
Illustrations by Joanna Hinton-Malivoire
Originated by Capstone Global Library Ltd.
Production by Victoria Fitzgerald
Printed and bound in China by South China Printing Company Ltd

15 14 13 12 11
10 9 8 7 6 5 4 3 2 1

Library of Congress Cataloging-in-Publication Data
Nunn, Daniel.
Shapes around us / Daniel Nunn.
p. cm.—(Math every day)
Includes bibliographical references and index.
ISBN 978-1-4329-5732-2 (hb)—ISBN 978-1-4329-5737-7 (pb)
1. Shapes—Juvenile literature. I. Title.
QA445.5.N86 2012
516'.15—dc23 2011013020

Acknowledgments
We would like to thank the following for permission to reproduce photographs: Dreamstime.com p.13 (© Raphotography); Shutterstock pp.4 left (© Africa Studio), 4 right (© Lori Sparkia), 5 left (© erperlstrom), 5 right (© Coprid), 7 (© Dmitriy Shironosov), 8 (© Chiyacat), 8 (© Tilo G), 8 (© Carlos Caetano), 8 (© akiyoko), 8 (© Jiang Hongyan), 8 (© Kristina Postnikova), 9 (© Beneda Miroslav), 11 (© Anna Chelnokova), 12 (© Jiri Hera), 12 (© Konstantin Yolshin), 12 (© Evgeny Karandaev), 12 (© Dmitry Naumov), 12 (© Swapan), 16, 17 (© Mariia Sats), 20, 21(© karamysh).

Cover photograph of a Palheiro Traditional thatched house, Santana village, Madeira reproduced with permission of Alamy (© STOCKFOLIO®).

Every effort has been made to contact copyright holders of any material reproduced in this book. Any omissions will be rectified in subsequent printings if notice is given to the publisher.

2
Printed in the United States 5657

Contents

Shapes Around Us 4

Circles 6

Squares 10

Rectangles 14

Triangles 18

Other Shapes 22

Index 24

Shapes Around Us

Let's look for shapes.
It's time to play!

How many shapes can you find today?

Circles

This is a circle.
Circles are round.

Look at this photo.
How many have you found?

Circles, circles, everywhere!

Is this window a circle?

No, it's a square!

Squares

1

4

Squares have
four sides, all
the same size!

2

3

How many squares are here?

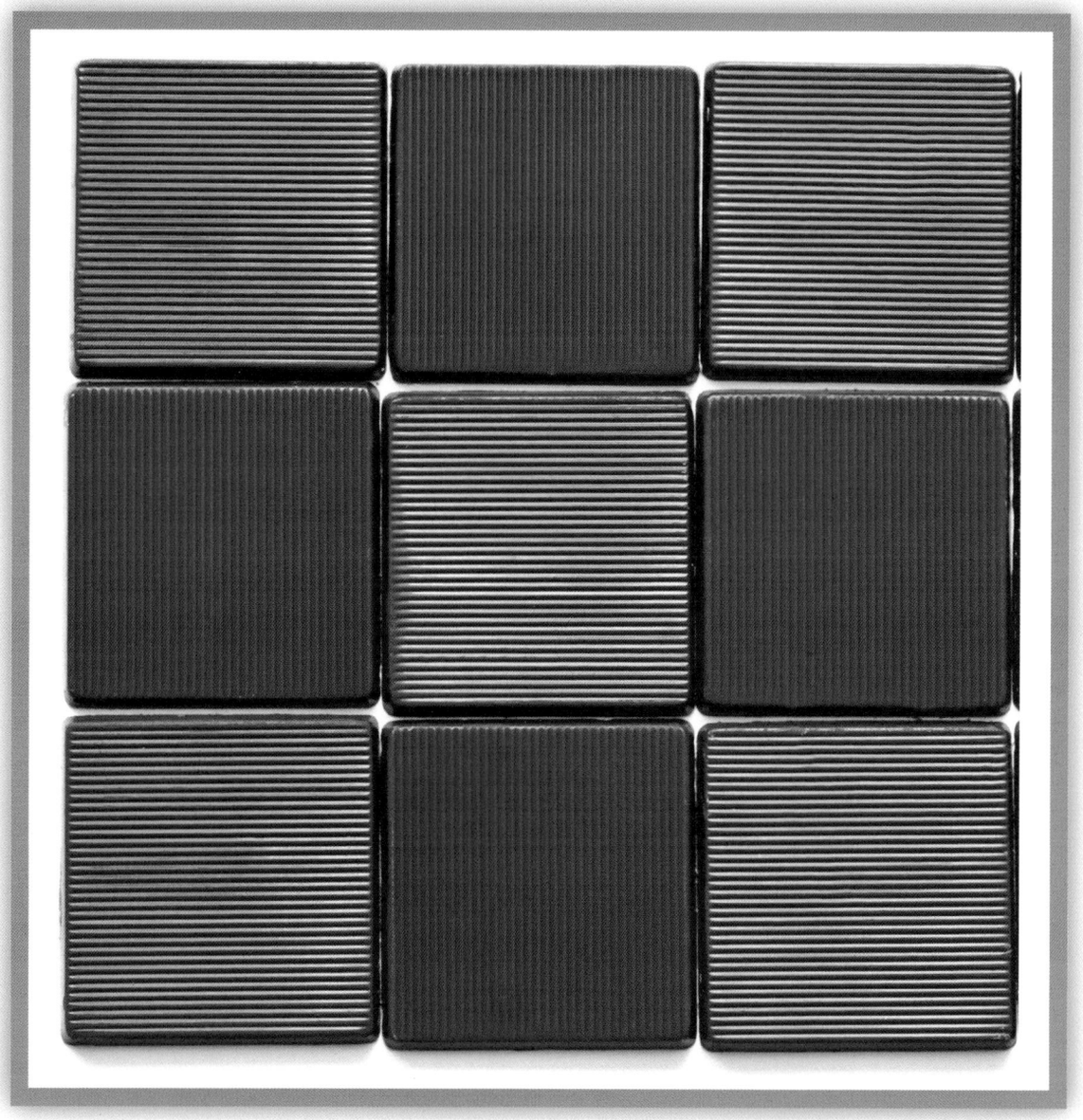

Look with your eyes!

Here are some more squares,
both big squares and small.

Are there squares on this cake?
Try and count them all.

Rectangles

long side

short side

A rectangle has four sides,
two short and two long.

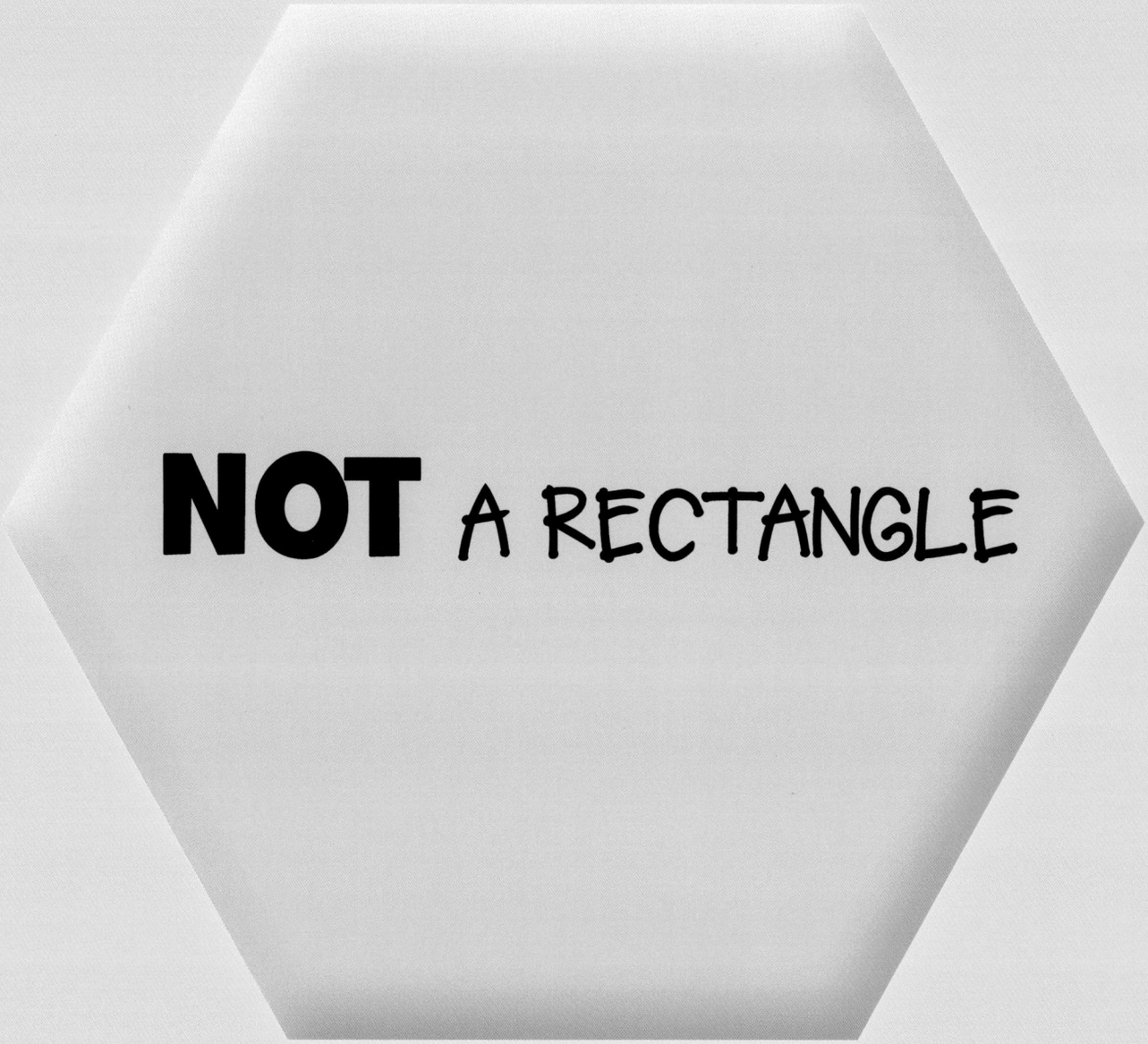

If you think it's got six sides,
I'm afraid you'd be wrong!

Can you see any rectangles by this front door?

I can see at least three, can you see any more?

Triangles

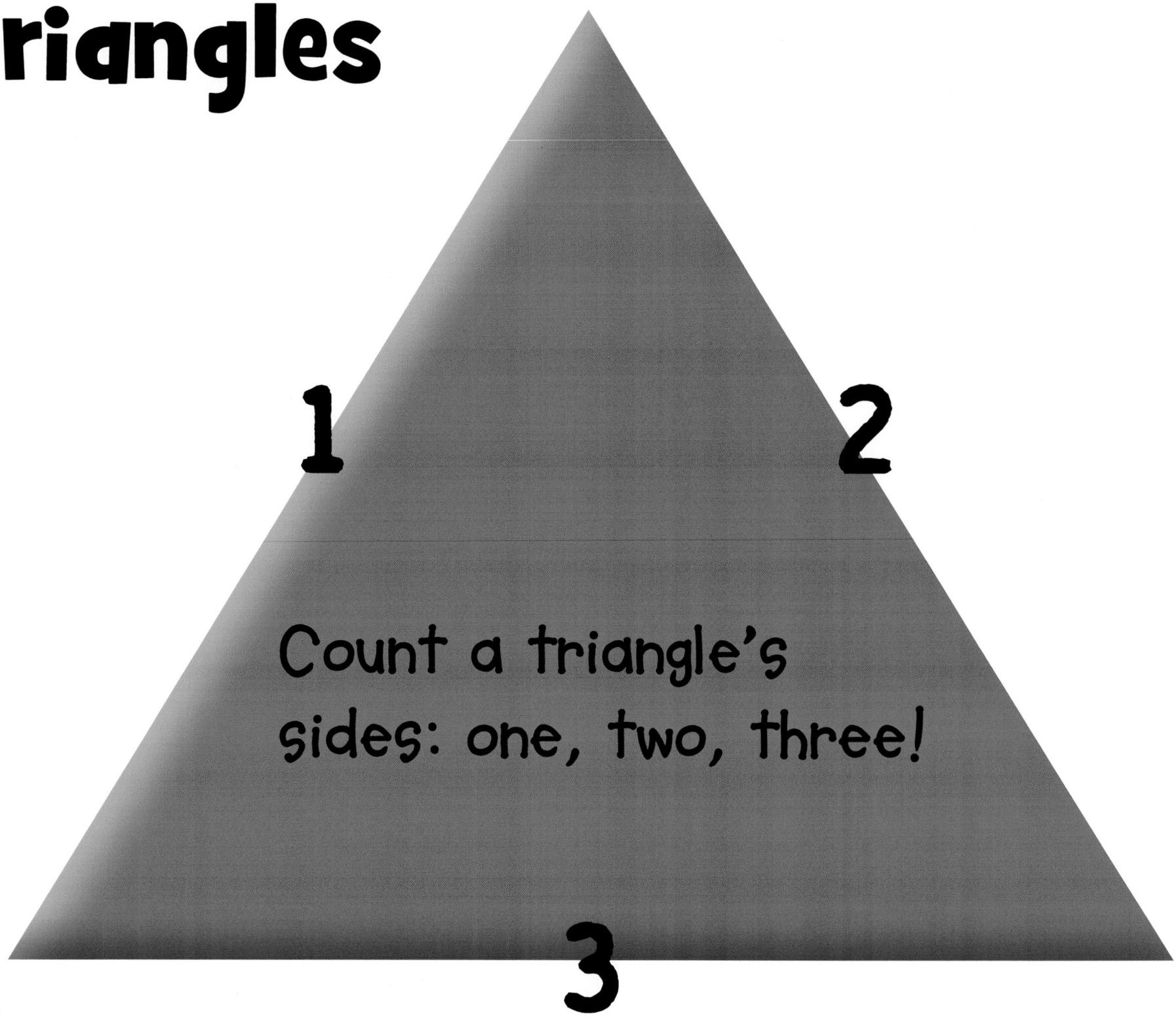

Count a triangle's sides: one, two, three!

How many points does it have?
Can you see?

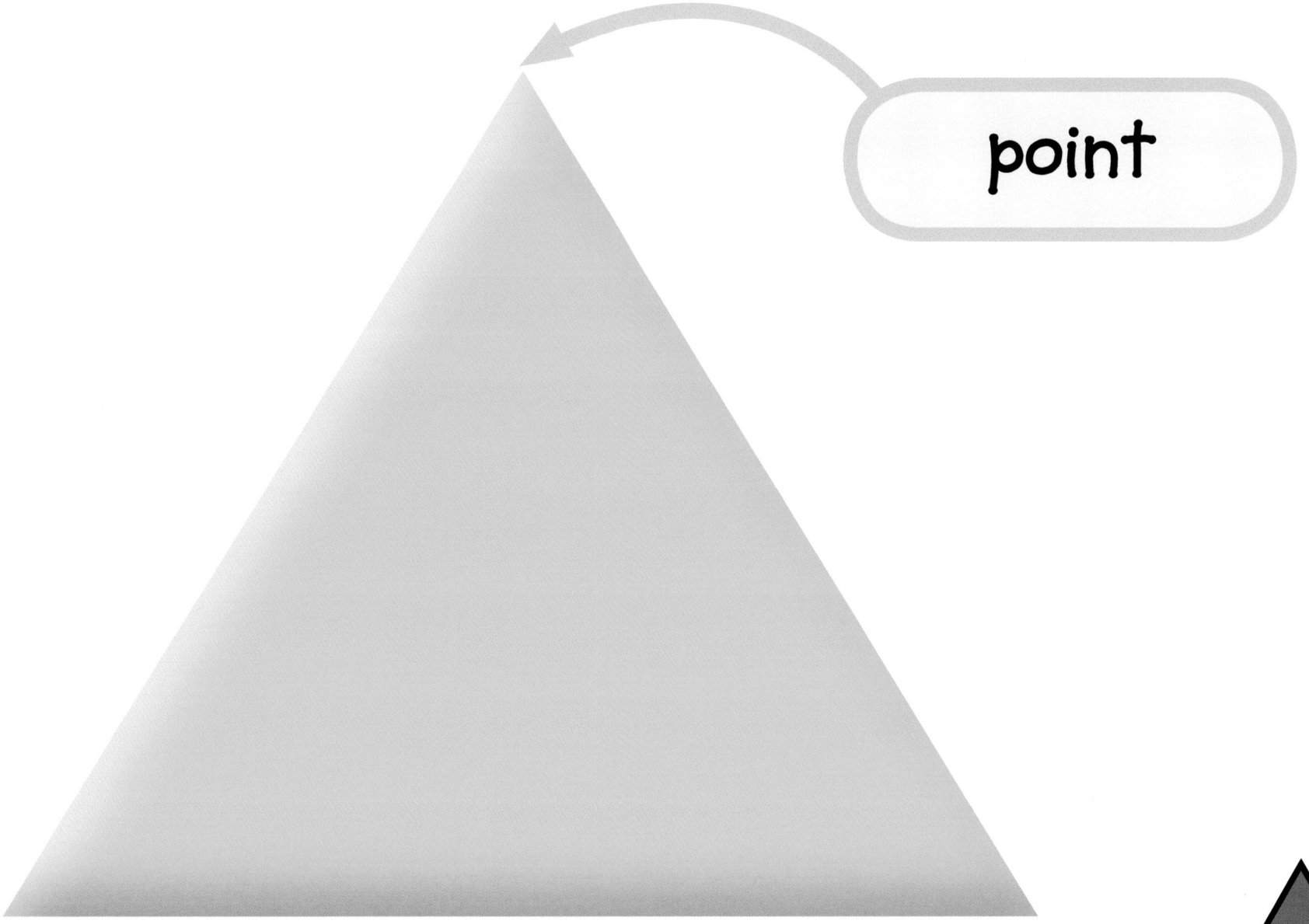

Look at this picture.
Are there triangles here?

If you found at least three,
then I'll give you a cheer!

Other Shapes

Are there other shapes, too?
Yes, of course there are!

Do you know the names
of these shapes?

If you do, you're a star...

(And a star is a shape too!)

Answers on page 24

Index

circles 6, 7, 8
diamonds 23
hexagons 15, 22
ovals 23
quiz 22, 23
rectangles 14, 16, 17
stars 22, 23
triangles 18, 19, 20, 21

Answer to question on page 22

Shape 1 is a hexagon.

Shape 2 is a star.

Shape 3 is a diamond.

Shape 4 is an oval.